Post Urbanism & ReUrbanism

Michigan Debates on Urbanism

Everyday Urbanism
New Urbanism
Post Urbanism & ReUrbanism

Series Editor, Douglas Kelbaugh

Edited by Roy Strickland

Designs for Ground Zero

Post Urbanism & ReUrbanism

Peter Eisenman
vs.
Barbara Littenberg and Steven Peterson

Michigan Debates on Urbanism   volume III

Post Urbanism & ReUrbanism
Michigan Debates on Urbanism: volume III

Published to record the debate staged on April 20, 2004.

The Michigan Debates on Urbanism were supported by a
grant from the Graham Foundation for Advanced Studies
in the Fine Arts.

Design: Christian Unverzagt with Martha Merzig at M1, Detroit
Typeset in HTF Gotham and OurType Arnhem Fine

The University of Michigan
A. Alfred Taubman College of Architecture + Urban Planning
2000 Bonisteel Boulevard, Ann Arbor, Michigan 48109-2069 USA

734 764 1300
734 763 2322 fax
www.tcaup.umich.edu

Printed and Bound in the United States of America

ISBN 1-891197-36-3

Distributed Arts Press
155 Sixth Avenue, 2nd Floor
New York, NY 10013 USA

212 627 1999
212 627 9484 fax

Contents

George Baird

George Baird is Dean of the University of Toronto's School of Architecture, Landscape and Design and a partner in Baird Sampson Neuert Architects in Toronto. He is the co-editor (with Charles Jencks) of *Meaning in Architecture*, the author of a book on Alvar Aalto, of *The Space of Appearance*, and the forthcoming *A New Theory of Public Space*.

The Michigan Debates on Urbanism

A year or so ago, Dean Douglas Kelbaugh asked me to write a letter of support for funding a project to launch a series of debates on urbanism in the United States today. I agreed to do so, since I liked the format that he proposed, combining public participation, intellectual gravitas, and engaged polemic. And I was sympathetic to his tripartite classifications of Everyday, New, and Post Urbanisms, on which I have heard him speak and which I have written about in *Building/Art* (University of Calgary Press, 2003). He has since added ReUrbanism to the typology.

Each debate was to have a proponent of one of the urbanisms and a respondent of a different persuasion. It is now a year later; the debates in question have occurred; and it is my pleasure to write a foreword to a series of publications that cover the debates. The expectations I held for the series have more than been fulfilled. Participation by both speakers and spectators has been lively, the level of intellectual discourse high, and the polemical stances of the factions represented well articulated.

But it seems to me that I – and the audiences at the University of Michigan – got a bonus from the series: one that is a byproduct of the specific combination of personalities participating. For example, two of the three debates are conducted by opponents who, in the course of the event, come to reveal powerful, personal shared sets of commitments to specific geographical locations, and intellectual lineages. In two of them, the anticipated format of proposition followed by commentary, is effectively superseded by one in which the presentation of the initial speaker constitutes as much a critique of the stance of the respondent as it does a position proposed for response. For me, these features of the debates give this publication a deepened intellectual significance.

A number of currents of thought in American urbanist discourse that usually remain well below the surface of public discussion here become startlingly – even poignantly – evident.

I did not expect, for example, that the conversation between Margaret Crawford and Michael Speaks would be so engagingly suffused by their palpable, long-standing, and mutual affection for the specific urban features of Los Angeles. They did indeed disagree on the plane of theory as the format of the debates required that they do, and no reader of this series of texts will doubt that they hold different positions. But it is clear as well that Speaks does not so much oppose Crawford's idea of "Everyday Urbanism" as find it an insufficiently efficacious tool for the address of the contemporary urban issues. And Crawford is eager to align herself with such younger generation theorists such as Speaks on the matter of the role of the automobile in future American urban form. As she puts it: "the idea of eliminating the automobile is just a dream and, for me, not even a good dream. I don't want to give up my automobile. The thing I miss most about Los Angeles is the parking and the driving," an opinion to which Speaks quickly assents.

A parallel conversation comprises the third debate, even if this one, between Barbara Littenberg and Steven Peterson on the one hand, and Peter Eisenman on the other, plays out according to a quite different dynamic. Littenberg and Peterson argue for what is labeled in Volume III of the *Michigan Debates* as "ReUrbanism," rather than argue against any putative "Post Urbanist" position that might – per Kelbaugh – be ascribed to Eisenman. And this is probably just as well, since Eisenman confesses that he isn't sure that he is an urbanist at all.

But here too, two powerful undercurrents suffuse the conversation. The first one, as in the first debate, is a place: the city of New York, for which all three speakers figures share a powerful affection. The second is the deep intellectual debt all three owe to their shared urban design mentor: the late Colin Rowe.

Eisenman begins by setting out his own classification of urbanisms operative in recent years, calling them "Arcadian," "Utopian" and Koolhaasian "junk space" respectively (he includes Littenberg/Peterson in the Arcadian category). But in a fashion which you may find as surprising as I did, Eisenman offers a nostalgic nod to the Arcadian group observing that "their idea was a wonderful notion of urbanity." He associates the "Utopian" category with modernism, but observes that "both of those positions...have been problematized by the failure of Modernism, and the idea that you can go backward in time. I don't think it is possible."

Then, having dismissed his first two categories, he characterizes the third one as: "what I call junk space, Rem Koolhaas' urban theories," and then dismisses it as well: "Junk space is not a project because it isn't critical, it's cynical..." Having thus dismissed all three, Eisenman presents several of his recent projects. Yet he attempts little linkage of the projects to the themes of the theoretical introduction with which he began, and which I have just summarized, limiting himself solely to efforts at "incorporating the possibility of negativity into new research in mathematics, biology, physics..." For their part, Littenberg and Peterson launch no theoretical introduction at all, save for the insistence I have already cited: that "multiple urbanisms" do not really exist, and instead that "urbanism is a condition."

They proceed directly to an extended descriptive/analytical account of their firm's own recent urban design proposals for the Lower Manhattan site of the World Trade Center – design proposals that preceded the later and better-publicized design competition won by Daniel Libeskind.

But once Eisenman's and Littenberg-Peterson's opening presentations are concluded, their debate becomes charged in complex ways. To start with, Eisenman commends Littenberg-Peterson's "beautiful plans," but he then goes on to claim that "the concept of a good plan is no longer alive." Littenberg and Peterson resist this historicization, but in doing so, they argue that an urban design method that has the capacity to "heal the city" does not depend on a tightly determined relationship of an overall urban design plan to the design for any specific building to be erected within it. Before long, the methodological idea of "healing the city" and the non-determinist relationship of urbanism to architecture posited by Littenberg-Peterson drive Eisenman to balk: "I don't accept that architecture and urbanism are separate." Yet Peterson persists, and the exchange ends with his insistent observation that "the city is a different kind of form."

In this fascinating exchange, it seems to me that one sees being played out all over again, the tense dialectic between the more-or-less ahistorical methods that had been formulated and propounded by Rowe, and the more-or-less teleological revisionisms to them that have been so persistently pursued by Eisenman in recent years. But all this notwithstanding, Eisenman's Michigan references to the "failure of Modernism"; his disparagement of Koolhaas' characteristic current methodologies; his only-lightly-theorized account of his own recent production; and his admiration (however guarded) for Littenberg-Peterson's "beautiful plans" to-gether have the intriguing effect of returning him more closely to the intellectual lineage of Rowe than he has been for some time.

This brings me to the remaining debate in the series. This one – between Peter Calthorpe and Lars Lerup – had in common with both of the other two a reunion of former academic colleagues. But the interchange between these two protagonists, unlike that between both of the other pairs, did not underscore how much they have basically in common. In fact, in this case, one senses an estrangement between former colleagues, rather than a rapprochement. This effect is sharpened by Calthorpe's opening presentation, which he begins by describing his disappointment that the New Urbanism (of which he was Dean Kelbaugh's designated proponent) has been less successful as a coalition of diverse groups ("for people to think comprehensively about our patterns of growth") and is instead better-known as a neo-traditional style. Understandably exasperated by the its stylistic foregrounding in its East Coast versions, Calthorpe also dismisses in advance many of the criticisms commonly made of it – including, along the way, a number of those implicit in Lars Lerup's subsequent presentation. It is in this sense that I tend to see Calthorpe's presentation as being as much a critique as a proposition. But this is not to say that it is not a proposition. On the contrary, his eloquent plea for a shift from the familiar parameters of new urbanism to a consideration of "the Regional City" is a refreshing and compelling address to the whole panoply of issues central to contemporary urbanism: political, economic, environmental, social, etc. And his insistence on the need to bring detailed design sensibilities even to such obdurate matters as traffic flow on arterial highways, within the overall urban field, cannot be too highly praised.

To Calthorpe's broad – if somewhat impatient – account of the current scene, and of his own projects within it, Lerup responded with an account of his own "outsider's" enduring fascination with the American "myth" of mobility as freedom. Using his current home town of Houston as his test case, he delivers an often caustic account of current urban failures: mono-functional land use, the degradation of the bayous, etc. – even summing them up, in a telling phrase, as "toxic ecologies." But Calthorpe challenges Lerup on what he sees as his excessive infatuation with the "myth," and presses him to go much further – and to do so propositionally. He is, for example, intrigued by Lerup's tantalizing account of the ecological potentials of flat roofs in a location such as Houston's.

I want to conclude my commentary with a crossover theoretical reference. Reading through this series of commentaries in sequence, I have found myself seeing Calthorpe's engaging combination of historical critique and ambitious urban proposal in a new and different light. To my surprise, it has reminded me again of Eisenman's complaint about Koolhaas' theory. Following on from the theory of Manfredo Tafuri (and of Tafuri's colleague Massimo Caccari), Eisenman labels Koolhaas' method "nihilistic and cynical." Instead, Eisenman insists, "To have a project... means in some way or other to be critical."

I would not have expected it when I endorsed the Michigan Debates a year ago, but it seems to me that one of its fruitful outcomes is a reading of the efforts of such avowedly "on-the-ground" urbanists such as Peter Calthorpe as important contemporary – if perhaps unwitting – exemplars of the powerful theoretical ideas of Tafuri that Eisenman has championed, and that he has (perhaps less successfully?) sought to emulate for so long.

Douglas Kelbaugh

Douglas Kelbaugh, Dean of Taubman College of
Architecture and Urban Planning at the University
of Michigan, has won a score of design awards and
competitions, organized and participated in thirty
design charrettes, and taught at eight architecture
schools in the US and abroad. In addition to writing
dozens of articles, he has edited and authored
several books, most recently *Repairing the
American Metropolis: Common Place Revisited.*

Preface

Let me start with a little geo-history of urbanism and of these debates in particular, especially some of its transatlantic ironies. Urban design and planning ideas have been ricocheting back and forth across the Atlantic Ocean for centuries. There was Williamsburg, transplanted from Europe in the 16th century; Oglethorpe's plan for Savannah in the 17th; and L'Enfant's plan for our nation's capital in the 19th century. Lewis Mumford once commented that the early twentieth century ideas of the Regional Plan Association of America were actually realized a half-century later in the British New Towns. America embraced Le Corbusier's Tower in the Park in the housing projects of its urban renewal program of the 1960s.

Now the Urban Task Force in the UK, headed by Lord Richard Rogers, is citing and promoting smart growth and New Urbanist ideas in an attempt to build over 60 percent of that country's new development on urban brownfield sites. What strange, unexpected architectural bedfellow Rogers is with a New Urbanist like Andres Duany.

And there's Colin Rowe, the influential urban design educator and writer. During the last third of the twentieth century he was a shuttle diplomat between European and US schools of architecture. His Cornell progeny could not be better represented in this book than by Steven Peterson, who studied under him, and by Barbara Littenberg, who was influenced greatly by him.

Later the influence of continental European philosophers like Jacques Derrida reached North American shores through critical practitioners like Peter Eisenman, who we are also very lucky to have as part of this debate.

The three urbanisms in this series are Everyday, New, and Post Urbanism. We heard from Margaret Crawford in the debate on Everyday Urbanism that if we looked more closely we could find redeeming qualities in the most mundane and ordinary places, even places we are taught to dislike, such as malls. Michael Speaks was articulate about the lack of aspiration in this bottom-up urbanism that was "too much bottom, not enough up."

We heard in the second debate that New Urbanism is a coalition that comes in more flavors than usually recognized. The West Coast version, including Calthorpe's Transit-Oriented Development and regional-scale planning, has a different social and physical sensibility than the Neo-traditional East Coast version associated with Seaside and Celebration, Florida. We also witnessed Lars Lerup, the shrewd observer and poetic commentator on the American landscape, be remarkably if grudgingly sympathetic to New Urbanism's more progressive and open-ended efforts. However, he emotionally points out that we Americans have always gone to immense expense to put distance between ourselves and then go to equally immense expense to overcome that distance. We literally and figuratively go to great lengths to disconnect and then reconnect ourselves and are hopelessly, fundamentally suburban in Lars' Swedish eyes.

Post Urbanism is more elusive, as it is much more driven by aesthetics than by normative principles. In some sense, it is anti-urban, much like postmodernist architecture tended to be anti-modernist. It strives to embody, accommodate, and express the contemporary forces of technology, culture, and "flow," the central concept of contemporary spatiality in David Leatherbarrow's words. Post Urbanism is avant-garde, and it has no choice but sooner or later to become post-avant-garde. It will be a daring act to follow, but followed it is sure to be in our increasingly media-saturated world.

In previous introductions I've placed the three urbanisms in a continuum, with New Urbanism in the middle. The field in which these three paradigms sit is market urbanism or ReUrbanism, which is less ideological and is represented at the high end by the best works of such firms as Peterson/Littenberg, as well as Machado/Silvetti, Rafael Moneo and Renzo Piano. At the low end is commercial architecture with its the default urbanism that we see in the countless arterial strips, office parks, and shopping malls of suburban America.

Let me offer one last cut on why these three urbanisms are inevitable developments, or redevelopments, in the human condition. During the Renaissance, the Italian architect Serlio described three kinds of architecture: comic, tragic, and satiric. Comic represented the everyday and ordinary, with all its humorous foibles and predictable, but seemingly important, trivialities. Tragic represented the heroic, destined-to-fail attempt to make a more perfect world. The satiric exposed and ridiculed human vice and folly. One might say Everyday Urbanism is like the comedic because it is rooted in the day-to-day, unpretentious life of everyday citizens. New Urbanism is like the tragic because it heroically, and perhaps vainly, strives for a more balanced and perfect world.

This leaves tonight's subject, Post Urbanism, aligned – perhaps not as neatly – with the satiric, because it can be scornful of empty, self-righteous or sentimental architectural pretense. Clearly not about the local and the everyday, it attempts to express the Zeitgeist. In fact, Post Urbanists are sometimes referred to as "the Zietgeisters."

This evening we are not only going to talk about Post Urbanism but ReUrbanism, a term I first heard from our own Robert Fishman. (If "Post Urbanism" and "ReUrbanism" stick, the *Michigan Debates on Urbanism* will have at least contributed two new terms to the lexicon.) ReUrbanism describes the positive redevelopment and revitalization of American cities that is now happening piecemeal – the loft conversions, the in-town malls, the art museums, the concert halls, and sports arenas. It might also be called old urbanism, or simply urbanism (to be done with all the prefixes). It's the type of urban design that Steven and Barbara both profess and practice. It is why they are in this debate, along with Peter, who is not sure he wants to be part of it or even sure, he has mentioned, that he believes in urbanism per se. I thank them both for subjecting themselves to academic, classification and for their willingness to debate Post Urbanism, a term with which neither of them identify.

Peter agreed to this because he is a game, loyal, upfront and outspoken person. I met him as a sophomore in my first architecture course on basic design. He was a great teacher, one of our favorites (along with Charles Gwathmey and Michael Graves). It was sort of a boot camp in which he turned our conventional values on their heads, stripping us of our inherited, bourgeois predilections. He convinced us that Corb's white buildings with pencil-thin black window sashes were not only heroic but beautiful, despite our suburban American sensibilities and despite the depressingly gray and grainy photographs in *Towards a New Architecture* to which he often referred. He was very persuasive, and my classmates and I have been struggling ever since with his mandate for a more pure and autonomous architecture. An equally large struggle has been with urbanism, a subject to which we now turn.

I would like to thank all the debater/writers, the moderator/editors, and the staff who worked hard on this project, but, alas, there are too many to name. I must, however, single out Keria Rossin for her patient typing, Christian Unverzagt and Martha Merzig for their thorough and thoughtful graphic design, Peter Knox for his DVD/video transfer, and George Baird, who took time out from his new job as Dean at the University of Toronto to write the Foreword. For their help on this volume, Larissa Babij of Eisenman Architects and the UM Art and Architecture Librarian Rebecca Price were both invaluable. I'd also like to acknowledge the Graham Foundation for their grant.

Peter Eisenman, principal in Eisenman Architects, has won numerous design awards, most recently the Venice Biennalle's Golden Lion for Lifetime Achievement. He has taught at Princeton, Harvard, Yale, Cambridge, and Ohio State as well as founding the Institute for Architecture and Urban Studies in New York. He is author of several books, including *House X, Fin diOu T Hous, Moving Arrows, Eros and Other Errors*, and *House of Cards*.

Thoughts on the World Trade Center

There are three major conditions in modern or contemporary urbanism. One is what I call the Arcadian impulse, which I think is represented by people like Leon Krier, Dimitri Porphyrios, Peterson/Littenberg, the New Urbanists, etc. I don't want to categorize them, but the general idea is a return to an idea of the city of the past, of the eighteenth and even nineteenth century.

The second I would call Utopian, which is that the world is never the same as the present and the future must always be better. Modernism was about the search for a utopia. I think both of those positions in one way or another have been problematized by the failure of Modernism. But the idea that you can go backward in time is, in any case, possible.

The third position is what I call a realist or cynical position. It can be categorized by Rem Koolhaas' urban theories of junk space. Koolhaas' position is an extreme one, brought about both by the Arcadian and the Utopian. In one sense it is not cynical but nihilistic. However, the notion of the "project," whether it is an urban project or an architecture project, means some form of reflection on the status quo, i.e., a critical view. The nature of that reflection is what separates the Arcadian from the Utopian, even though they are both in one sense failed projects. Junk space, on the other hand, is not a project because it is not critical, it is what Massimo Cacciari calls nihilism fulfilled.

The difference in these reflections occurred in Rome in the late eighteenth century between Nolli and Piranesi's view of the urban condition. Nolli's idea was a way of looking at his present that was different than in the past. He was one of the first people to do figure/ground maps, and clearly the impetus of what one would call New Urbanism, or the Arcadian, deals with that moment in time when the Nolli map became an urban icon.

The other icon is Piranesi's Campo Marzio map, which has no unified idea of what a city would be about. In fact it confounds the notion of the city as a linear narrative. It has no streets; it has no actual time because part of it is the Rome of the eighteenth century, and part of it is the imperial Rome of the first and second centuries. Part of the Piranesi map has monuments from the first and second centuries that are moved in different locations, part of it has monuments supposedly from a Rome that never existed. Thus, there is a condition of fiction as well as what I would call chance, the arbitrary, a mixing of reality and fiction into some arbitrary brew.

The difference between the Nolli map and the Piranesi map is significant, in fact, I could have done the lecture tonight with just those two images because they are what makes a fundamental and important difference.

For me, Piranesi was the beginning of the modern critical project, the project that suggested that there was no single time, that there was no single hierarchy or relationship between signs and their signifiers. This idea carried through from the Piranesi project to the present.

But there are three issues that define the critical project in our moment in time that are important. First is the notion of the metaphysics of presence, which is the dominant mode of discourse which has placed architecture in a situation in which it is seen to be static, stable, unified, rather than fragmentary, continuous, and complex.

It seems to me that 1968 was a watershed time, with Venturi's book, *Complexity and Contradiction* with Derrida's *Of Grammatology*,

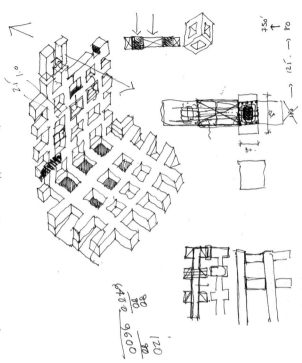

1 ↗ Conceptual sketch by Peter Eisenman.

Peter Eisenman

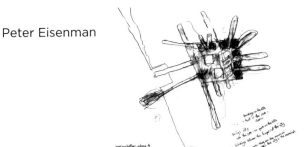

2 ↗ Early team sketch for Memorial Square concept with "fingers" stretching from the site out into the city.

3 ↗ Site sketch incorporating shadows of the fallen towers into the design.

4 ↖ Site plan situated in lower Manhattan context.

5 ↙ Axonometric of red brick "fingers" and shadows of the original towers.

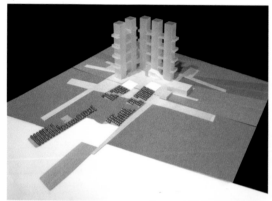

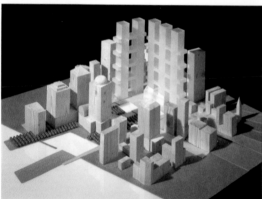

Tafuri's *Theories in History*, Rossi's *The Architecture of the City*. All of them in one way or another attacked the notion of an historical and static notion of the city.

Architecture is supposed to be the locus of the metaphysics of presence. If we question that notion, if we are singular and autonomous because we are the only discipline that must place, and if we are to be critical, we must displace at the same time. Placing and displacing I call the becoming unmotivated of the metaphysics of presence. I think the relationship between signs and stable language has been questioned. What was called a transcendental signifier is no longer a believable notion. That would involve becoming unmotivated of the sign. This is a second project.

The third is the becoming unmotivated of the subject. The subject is still physically the same, but in terms of gender, in terms of color, in terms of ethnicity, in terms of psychology, we are all very different people. The life sciences, natural sciences, physics, mathematics – have changed enormously. We no longer have a mathematics of form as known through Rudolf Wittkower and Colin Rowe; we have a calculus of form. We have changed from the analogic models of a Frank Gehry to the digital models of a Greg Lynn. Those digital models are different from any previous models because they rely on a non-stable, non-static condition of origin. Today there is no single condition of origin. Whether they were Rowe's models, a semiological model, linguistic models, or diagrammatic models, they all relied on a stable condition of origin. The models called abstract machines, which people like Greg Lynn and others are working on, no longer require in their digital calculus a condition of wholeness to begin working.

6-7 ↗ Model, views from southeast.

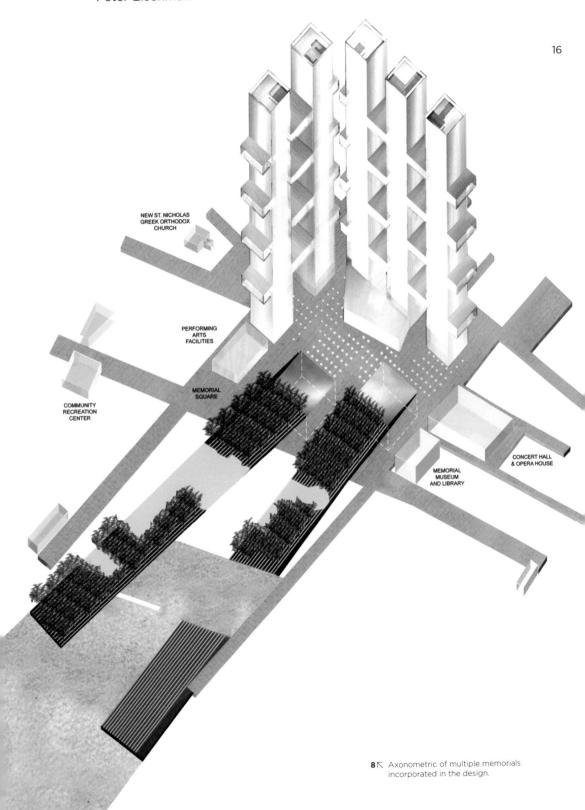

NEW ST. NICHOLAS
GREEK ORTHODOX
CHURCH

PERFORMING
ARTS
FACILITIES

COMMUNITY
RECREATION
CENTER

MEMORIAL
SQUARE

CONCERT HALL
& OPERA HOUSE

MEMORIAL
MUSEUM
AND LIBRARY

8↖ Axonometric of multiple memorials
incorporated in the design.

9 ↖ Site plan.

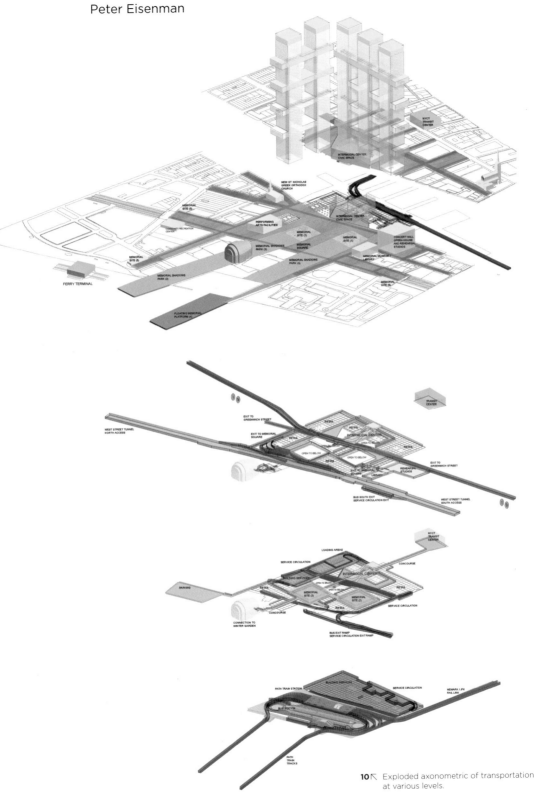

10 ⬉ Exploded axonometric of transportation at various levels.

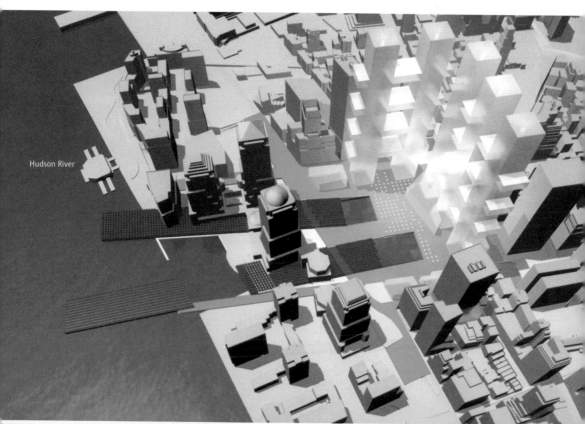

Hudson River

11-12 ↗ Rendering at sunset, view from Hudson River
(courtesy dbox.com); Axonometric, view from above.

13-14↘ Final presentation model, view from southwest; View from west.

The world has changed enormously. The tools available to us today are radically changed. Leatherbarrow talks about the notion of flow: The difference in flow today from the past is that flow is seen today as an integral part of matter. It is no longer separate from matter, and the conception of space and time as matter/flow as an integral proposition changes what is possible in the built environment.

Unfortunately, today architecture is not made up of those people who challenge the status quo. The only histories that we know, however, are histories that are made of those challenges. The rest return architecture to normalcy. The ebb and flow of things from Brunelleschi, Alberti, Bramante, Serlio, Palladio, Borromini, Piranesi, Rainaldi, down to the present, have always concerned the challenge to the status quo. Challenging the status quo means to have a critical project. It also means that criticality has to do with the possibility with what I would call an enfolded negativity. It is not just utopian; it has to also contain its opposite, its shadow, both psychologically and in physical terms.

The difference between the Modernist project today and the Arcadian project lies in this area of an enfolded negativity. There is no enfolded negativity that I can see in the Arcadian project. The Modernist project still relies on the negativity that was first put forward by people like Walter Benjamin, Nietzsche, Adorno, Heidegger, and others.

Much of contemporary science has been built on that skepticism, which incorporated the possibility of negativity into new research in mathematics, biology, physics and other disciplines.

15-16 ↗ Final presentation model, view from northeast; Aerial view of scheme collaged into New York cityscape (rendering courtesy dbox.com).

23

One of the most important things one can do as an architect is complexes of buildings on an increasingly large scale that probably approach urbanism. If matter is now animated with forces which are integral to matter, than the space between buildings can no longer be just left over. We can no longer have geometric mathematical formalism. Instead there will be calculus formalisms which deal with much more complex relationships between space, time and buildings.

The shift from the analogic to the digital, is the most important revolution that has occurred in architecture in a long time. When we have algorithms written for architects, about architecture in space and time, we are going to see very different things than are being produced by the Gehrys, the Hadids and the Lynns today.

They are, like me, the endgame of what I call the society of the spectacle. The last blow to the society of the spectacle was 9/11 when reality overtook media. We could never make a science fiction film like that. When reality overtook media, you realize that being in New York near the event, the Heideggerian notion of being there, became more important than seeing it on media. For me, being there re-established architecture and urbanism as an important condition of culture as we move forward.

17-18 ↘ Night view from Hudson River; View from northeast, Brooklyn Bridge in foreground. Renderings courtesy dbox.com.

19 ↖ Rendering from Hudson River, view from northwest. Courtesy dbox.com.

20 ↗ Rendering from Greenwich Street, looking south. Courtesy dbox.com.

Steven Peterson, a founding partner of Peterson/Littenberg, has a forty-year involvement with urban design and city planning. He was Assistant Chief Deputy Architect for Milton Keynes New Town in England, executive director of the Institute for Architecture and Urban Studies in New York, and director of the Syracuse University Post-Professional Program in Architecture in Florence, Italy.

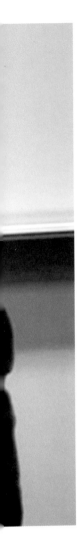

Urban Design in Lower Manhattan

I want to shift your mind and thoughts about this. First, I need to say this: We are not New Urbanists, nor is our work Arcadian. It is not about new types of suburban development and it is not about the rural countryside, which is what Arcadian means. We do urban design in central cities and have spent our entire careers involved with design in existing cities. Barbara and I believe urban design is an important field in itself. It addresses characteristics of scale, horizontal extension, and multiplicity of form which make it different from architecture. I also have to disagree with both Peter's and Doug's premise that there are multiple urbanisms. Their sense of stylistic categories suggests that the city is a thing that can be easily changed and transformed in a short time.

While cities do evolve, grow, and change, they are also made of fundamentally constant elements – spatial and formal ingredients, which are immutable, that don't change. Barbara and I believe that urbanism is a condition, one that has been fundamentally the same since civilization started.

Our position in this series is being called ReUrbanism. It is an apt description of what we do. It also relates to the rediscovery of urban form in the late 60s. At that time, architects began to realize that the city could be seen as an alternative, new formal paradigm. One which stood in opposition to many of modern architecture's destructive proscriptions: its cult of the new, its object building dependency, its anti-urbanistic super-blocks and its rejection of the street.

Urban design became a new field. It became an important instrument to undo the destruction of urban renewal and to re-urbanize the American city. Urban design was

2 ↗

not conceived as architecture itself, but as a premise for it. Urban design addresses the larger patterns of city, of neighborhood and of public space, which jointly serve as the context and the enabler of architecture.

Tonight, we will show you the different scales of urban design. Barbara will show you our specific proposals for reconstructing the World Trade Center site. I will show you the larger framework of our 1994 Lower Manhattan Urban Design Plan.

On the left is a photograph of Lower Manhattan in 2002, at the time we did the Mayor's Plan.[1] You can see that the World Trade Center is gone. On the right, the aerial survey is taken from 1994, when we did the urban design plan.[2] It shows the World Trade Center still in place.

Lower Manhattan is a city based on a seventeenth-century plan. It is also one of the most concentrated, intense, astonishing modern cities in the world today. It has an historical organic plan similar to Florence or some European city, but it is built out as this extraordinary collection of tall modern buildings. The succession of architectural reconstructions over the years has not altered the original plan.

The basic issue here (and this is one of the reasons that we are different from the New Urbanists) is that we accept the premise and necessity of tall buildings as an urban type. This is clearly the key to the extraordinary achievement of the American city, the combination of the functional and the fantastic: the gridded ground plan of streets, blocks, and parks, which are topped by a skyline of towers.

Lower Manhattan is emblematic of this, because building was contained and forced upwards by the two rivers. In the 1980s,

4 ↗

3 ↗

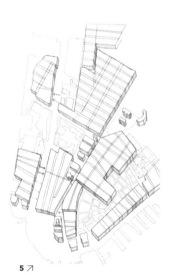

5 ↗

every city in North America attempted to emulate Lower Manhattan. This was called somewhat derisively the Manhattanization of the American city.

The figure/ground plan[3] and the view of Wall Street office buildings[4] illustrate this dual condition. The plan represents the extended arrangement at the ground, with its complex and interesting spatial network. This is, if you will, the traditional city or the horizontal city. Rising above it is the city of towers, the vertical city, with its own dynamic and visual interest. This dialectic is the essence of contemporary urbanism. It is composed of opposites; the plan and the view, the horizontal and the vertical, the old and the new, the object and the void. You can go on...the traditional and the contemporary.

So what's the problem? The problem in 1994 in Lower Manhattan was that, after the '93 bombing of the World Trade Center and the stock market crash of '87, there was a 46 percent office vacancy rate. The tenants had left. The city was virtually empty. Part of the problem was, like all American city centers, almost no one lived there. All the buildings were offices at that time. It was not a 24-hour city. The only housing of any significance was in Battery Park City on the far left of the plan. There were approximately twelve thousand people living in all of Lower Manhattan. It was a commuter center.

At its peak, 150,000 to 200,000 people came in to the city and back out every day. At five o'clock it was empty. It's a beautiful physical place, but it didn't exist as a living urban environment.

What can you do as an urban designer to resolve this problem? First, look at the existing conditions. Most of the building sites outside of Battery Park City are already occupied by very tall and often beautiful buildings.

Unless you're willing to tear down those buildings, you have to look at the situation from a different perspective and perhaps from multiple directions. A clean slate is not possible or desirable. One direction is to broaden the uses and drastically increase the housing opportunities so there is an ongoing vital city that is resilient to market swings in commercial real estate.

So, one objective was to get more people to live there, the other was to not tear down the older office buildings with the small floor plates. Changing the zoning and providing economic incentives could stimulate residential conversions in the existing office buildings. With increased residential population, the streets would be activated and the whole urban environment improved at the ground level. The horizontal city of the street could develop new vitality, more retail, entertainment, services and cultural uses.

In addition to these use changes, the city's pattern of streets needs to be improved and better integrated. The city was developed haphazardly in different landfill sections. The diagram of blocks shows how each subsequent district was cut off from the other.[5] The whole urban texture is a disjointed series of separate grids. There are only two streets in Lower Manhattan that run from river to river and there are no cross-town streets in the Wall Street core.

If you follow the diagrams of blocks from left to right and imagine trying to drive or walk across, you can see the physical problem. Beginning at Battery Park City, the primary grain of the urban fabric is oriented cross town, east-west but it hits the enormous gap of the West Side

Highway, which is a limited access road with a concrete barrier down the middle. Then, on the other side of the highway the grain of the blocks runs in the opposite direction, north-south. Then east of Broadway, the main spine, there are virtually no street alignments. It is not possible for somebody to walk this eight hundred feet from the only residential area into the Wall Street core and interact, shop or go to dinner there.

It's an incomplete, dysfunctional network. You can put as many people as you want in Battery Park City but they will never cross these barriers to enliven the central office area.

In the overall design plan for Lower Manhattan,[6] our urban design intervention proposed three things.

First, reknit the disjointed urban fabrics. These are shown in areas of dark red blocks, one of which is this connection between Battery Park City and the business center.

Second, create two new residential/mixed-use neighborhoods around newly made public spaces. One is Greenwich square on the lower left. The other is the long Fulton Square in the upper middle of the plan.

Third, redesign the two major north-south roads to integrate them into the city street system as urban boulevards. Then connect them at the bottom of the island into a completed loop.

From this overall view,[7] the results look simple, but it involves complex and intricate planning in many places to reweave the overall public space network into a new unified framework. It is interesting that this design can be drawn and represented without specific architectural buildings.

Now let me show you some of the specifics of the plan.

6 ↗

9 ↘

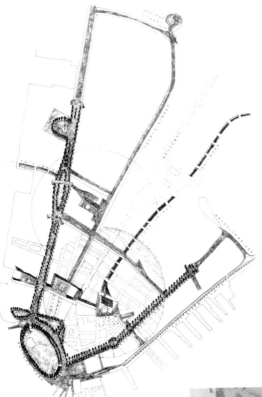

8 ↗

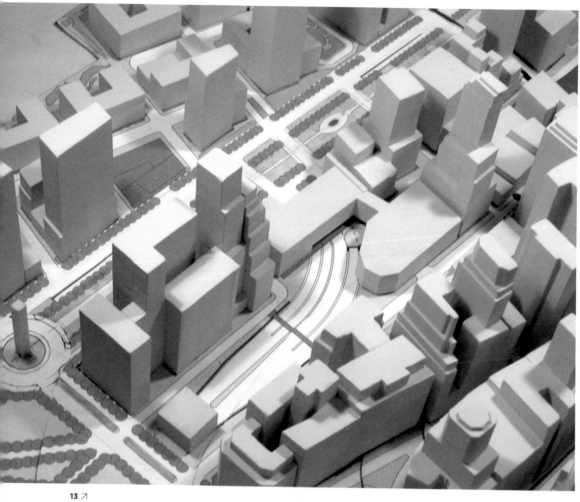

13 ↗

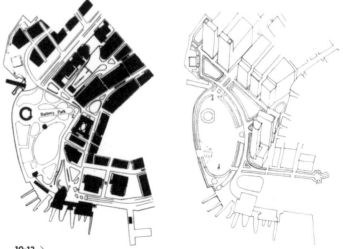

10-12 →

14 ↗

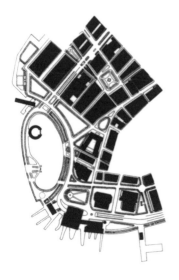

First, the plan diagram of the new road network shows how the two existing edge roads, West Street and Water Street can be transformed into urban boulevards that are attractive and serve as positive assets to the city.[8] They are linked together, at the end of the island, in a new oval drive at Battery Park so that they connect into a loop around the downtown.

The accompanying view of this new West Street Boulevard[9] is from eight years later as we developed it in greater detail for our World Trade Center proposal. It evolved into a pedestrian centered promenade like a very wide Park Avenue. The 200-foot wide highway, which once was a barrier, could become a prestigious location, with a linear park, that joined the city together.

The proposed new oval at Battery Park would produce a clear new symbolic space, while smoothly accommodating the connection of the two boulevards.[10-12] The current park is an accretion of haphazard elements. A stronger northern street wall to the space is also proposed to better define a clear city edge and provide valuable new building sites.

Just north of Battery Park, behind this new street wall, is the entrance to the existing Brooklyn Battery Tunnel, which is shown here in model and plan.[13,14] This area is the key to repairing the street linkages across the lower part of the island and to making a new residential neighborhood. You can see the roads curving down under, where a whole block of the city is missing. The rupture in the urban fabric is obvious, cutting off any possible connections across it.

The plan[15] and model[16] of our urban design proposal shows the new residential park, "Greenwich Square," built over the tun-

nel entrance. Surrounding it are new 40-story housing towers arranged to define the space.

The positive results are obvious. A new public park becomes the focus for apartments to house 3,500 new residents. These new blocks re-establish the urban fabric of the new neighborhood and link it to the surrounding city. This repaired street fills in the gap and integrates Battery Park City into the downtown.

Our final proposal for Lower Manhattan was part of our work on the Mayor's Plan done later in 2002, when we added a new development on the East River to balance Battery Park City.

In this plan and rendering you can see a new extension of the city projected out into the East River.[17,18] This provides for more residential on the East Side of the city as well as recreational facilities that are needed by the whole downtown, and a variety of cultural uses that cannot be inserted into the existing city fabric.

Because of the sensitive aquatic environment and depth of the East River, this cannot be landfill. The water will actually flow under the buildings and parks and will be seen throughout the area in open channels, ponds and pools. The plan extends each major east-west street of the existing city fabric out over the water into a new alternating rhythm of public parks and urban blocks.

The central boat basin space, illustrated in the rendering, sits at the east end of Wall Street. Waterfront promenades and terraced public gardens rise up from it onto the roofs of parking and retail. The area contains four thousand dwelling units, a location for the City Opera, the Cirque du Soleil, parking, shops, ferry terminals at the ends of streets, a soccer

15-16 ↗

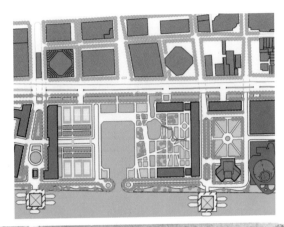

21-20 ↗

19 ↗

22 ↗

field, heliport, and a site for the new Guggenheim museum, which is floated out over the water like Corbu's Venice hospital.

I will end with a couple of observations about urbanism. One is about towers in a city fabric. The other is the necessity of two-sided streets.

The first is that the forms of "traditional city" and "contemporary architecture" are not mutually exclusive. It is false to assume that the context of city form inhibits architectural expression. Clearly, it is not true in Lower Manhattan. Historically, this dense city has had to combine streets and blocks with towers. The city's urban form has been a provocation for architectural expression. This is illustrated in two existing buildings of different styles. In each, the horizontal street architecture is dynamically combined with an almost independent vertical architecture in the air.

The base of the neo-classical Standard Oil Building twists along down Broadway to form the curved edge of Bowling Green.[19] On top, the tower emerges as a pure geometric form, a freestanding symbol. But it does not face Broadway as expected. Instead it is rotated to the side to connect down through a slot to the street on the short elevation.

This is a picture of the Art Deco City Fire & Trust Co. building.[20] The plans of the building[21] at various levels show how this marvelous massing is constructed out of series of inventive geometric forms. The whole ensemble twists and turns up into the air out of its imbedded triangular block to emerge in the pure square tower.

The second observation is about the nature of a successful urban street. This aerial view of Fifth Avenue looking north from Wash-ington Square up into Central Park illustrates this point.[22] In a dense city like Manhattan, a street has to be two-sided to work. It must also be backed up on either side by a depth of city blocks that feed into it and activate it. An urban street has to be two-sided to sustain active retail and to be defined as a contained, comfortable spatial room to walk in. It is also clear from the photo that the architecture along it can also vary enormously. You can have both the Empire State building and five-story town houses on the same street. This seems so obvious and simple, but it was almost universally ignored in all the designs for the World Trade Center site.

Barbara Littenberg is a founding partner of Peter-
son/Littenberg Architecture & Urban Design and
visiting professor at Yale School of Architecture.
Since 1979, she has been responsible for the firm's
award-winning design work ranging from private
houses to urban design projects. The firm was an
invited entrant into the international competition for
the World Trade Center Site.

Proposal for the World Trade Center

Having done the 1994 study that Steven just showed, we began work in 2002 feeling both familiar and enamored with the complex, multiple urban fabrics of Lower Manhattan. We also felt well versed in its history and underlying structural and financial difficulties. We followed a specific methodology of urban design that assumes city design is a necessary prior condition to architectural design. Manhattan itself was to be taken as the model for the reconstruction of the World Trade Center site – to be interpreted and extended as idea and typology of an enduring city form. The final World Trade Center site plan should be a child of Manhattan; it should physically embrace the tragedy of 9/11 – the loss of life and of iconic structures – by weaving the memory of this event into the very fabric of our city so that New York could move forward.

This is an aerial view of the ten million square foot World Trade Center office complex.[1] And here is a model of the site as we found it after the tragedy.[2] Although described as sixteen acres, the urban void including surrounding streets is actually thirty-four acres, a huge expanse in the densest of cities. Notice that the geometry of the street system surrounding the site is curious. The north-south perpendicular grid that extends north via Church Street and Broadway collides with the diagonal grid generated by Greenwich and Washington Streets, which parallel the Hudson River. Compositionally, the World Trade Center complex was oriented exclusively on the orthogonal north-south grid – the South Tower as a southern visual terminus for the merging of Greenwich Street and West Broadway, and the North Tower axially placed in the middle of Dey Street to the east, which leads to the heart of the Wall Street district.

1↗

As consultants to the Lower Manhattan Development Corporation beginning in April 2002, we began to analyze and test an exhaustive array of possible arrangements of public space, blocks, and streets – the ingredients of the public realm that is the essence of New York urbanism.[3] We organized the schemes typologically according to predominant street and space orientation characterized as "orthogonal" and "diagonal." Some schemes were generated independent of what went before, others retained elements such as the tower footprints. All had major public memorial space – some located within the original sixteen acres, others created by reclaiming space over West Street. In all cases, the program was the same, to replicate what had been lost with new cultural and museum space.

From these we developed two projects which were included in the first public offering in July 2002. The first was predominantly a "diagonal" scheme uniting the new buildings and the World Financial Center with a major memorial space and the east-west extension of Fulton and Cortlandt Streets.[4,5] Greenwich Street was extended through the site to reconnect to its southern part, which was cut off by the Yamasaki plan, and a new park was proposed across from St. Paul's Chapel in the northeast corner.

The second project was an "orthogonal" scheme, respecting the footprint outline of the former towers.[6,7] We learned a great deal from this first attempt as we proceeded to the next round of projects – the so-called Innovative Designs for the World Trade Center, which would be solicited from an international group of renowned designers.

Thinking changed a great deal during the first six months after 9/11. Initially the idea

2 ∠

45

3 ↘

Orthogonal Grids	Orthogonal Squares	Diagonal Grids	Diagonal Squares	Footprint Squares	Fulton Linear Park	Courtyard Blocks

Promenade

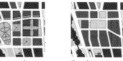
East/West Park (A)

Fulton Park

Park (A)

Orthogonal

Precinct (North-South Park)

Courtyard

Promenade (Footprints Open)

East/West Park (B)

Plinth

Park (B - Footprints Open)

Diagonal (Plan Prepared by the students of Michael Schwarting, NYIT)

Precinct (North-South Park, Footprints Open)

Block (A)

East/West Park (C)

Park (C - Footprints Open)

Precinct (East-West Galleria)

Block (B)

4-5 ↗ Memorial Park
West Street Partial Tunnel

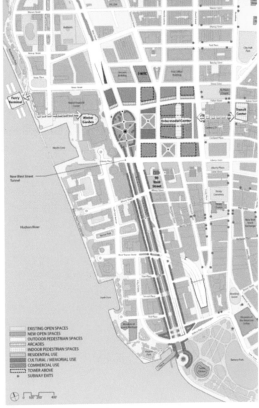

6-7 ↗ Memorial Promenade
West Street Tunnel (to Vesey Street)

EXISTING OPEN SPACES
NEW OPEN SPACES
OUTDOOR PEDESTRIAN SPACES
INDOOR PEDESTRIAN SPACES
ARCADES
RESIDENTIAL USE
CULTURAL / MEMORIAL USE
COMMERCIAL USE
TOWER ABOVE
* SUBWAY EXITS

of replacing the world's tallest building on this site was abhorrent to just about everybody. It would be the ultimate act of hubris and simply not an appropriate response to what had happened, the meaning of which remained unfathomable. We felt strongly that to replan the site as multiple, smaller venues and not one massive architectural project, was a far more sensitive way to restore lower Manhattan.

Further, we wished to remedy the gigantism of the World Trade Center superblock and what we believed were the fallacies in this kind of planning. During its troubled history, it was an inhospitable neighbor in an emerging residential district. Owned and operated by an interstate agency – the Port Authority of New York and New Jersey – it had its own governance and police force. Outside the jurisdiction of the City of New York, it was an isolated, unresponsive island, a bit like a Vatican City planted in lower Manhattan.

I would like to share the thinking that led to our specific proposal. The plan drawing of our project[8] and the plan of the World Trade Center[9] are to the same scale. For orientation, Vesey Street is the east-west boundary at the north. St. Paul's Chapel, that witnessed so much of the event and gave shelter to so many of the rescue workers, is at the northeast corner. Church Street is the eastern boundary. Liberty Street is the southern, culminating to the west in the main entrance to Battery Park City South. West Street, widened to the specifications of a now defunct Interstate Highway route, is the large space to the west distancing the World Financial Center complex.

Although few had much affection for the "Twin Towers" when they stood, as time passed a kind of nostalgia for them set in. Their loss on the skyline resulted in a public longing for an equivalent iconic replacement. The near impossibility of leasing space in a new building above the fiftieth floor, especially at that location, was generally understood. Could one really contemplate building the world's tallest building?

As the towers became part of the lore of the city, Steven and I came to believe that the memory of their physical presence should be woven into the new plan for the site. We were convinced that the correct venue for a meaningful memorial was the unchanging realm of permanent urban structure: public space, garden, an amphitheater, and a boulevard. Secular buildings cannot express sacred sentiments. Any specific commercial work of architecture will by definition be subject to obsolescence, change and reinterpretation. The memorial must remain a constant, integral part of the public realm, a timeless spatial element in the larger urban design plan with an immutable public stature equivalent to Central Park, Washington Square or Park Avenue.

This is an enlarged site plan.[10] Recall Steven's final image looking south down Fifth Avenue to its origin in Washington Square Park. Similarly, Lexington Avenue begins at Gramercy Park, Madison Avenue at Madison Square, and so on. This presents an important New York model – memorable civic open spaces are located in clear relationship to the long vistas established by major north-south avenues. Our plan honors the World Trade Center site by placing the primary memorial garden at the confluence of Greenwich Street and West Broadway reinforcing the primary Manhattan grid. The axial alignment of the South Tower with these two streets is symbolically replaced with an iconic void.

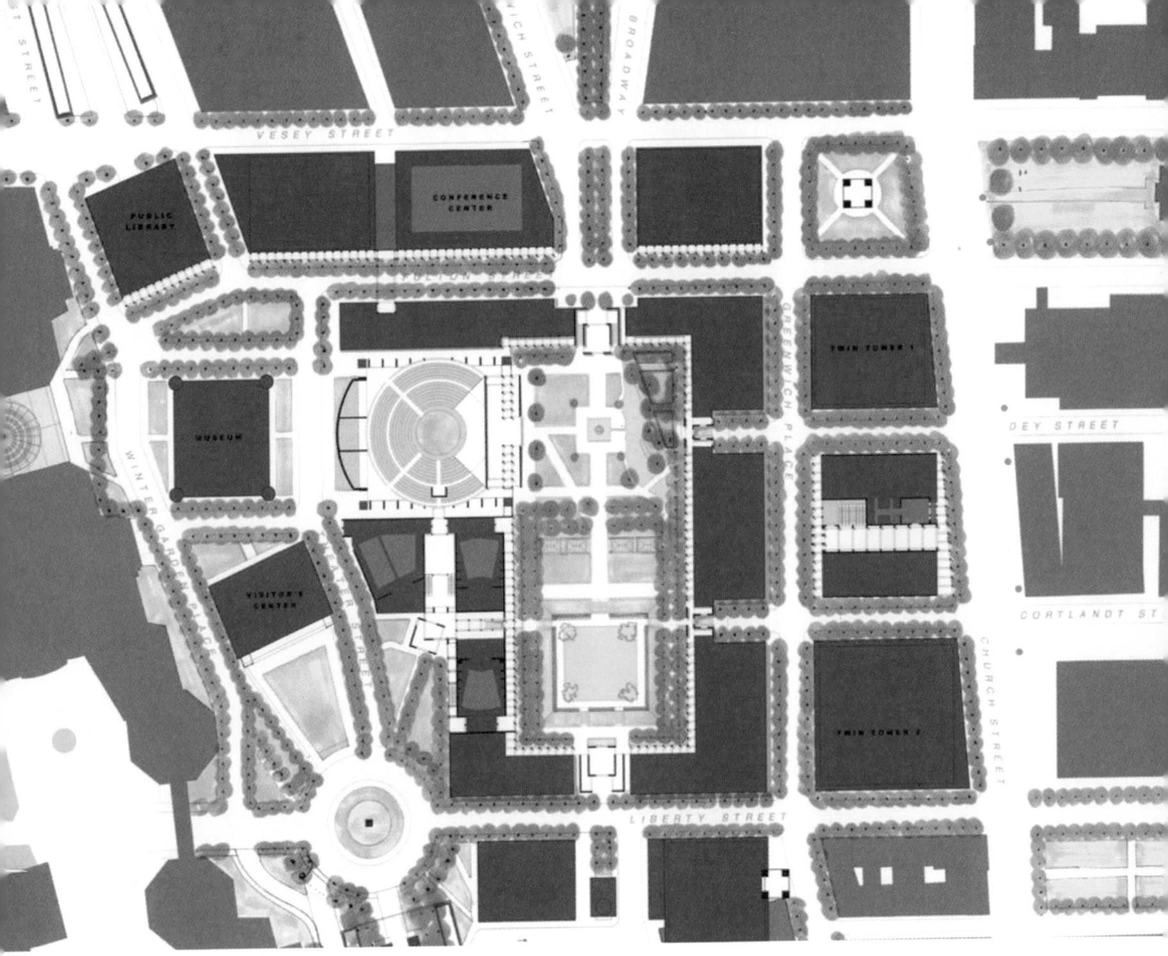
VESEY STREET
BROADWAY
CONFERENCE CENTER
PUBLIC LIBRARY
MUSEUM
VISITOR'S CENTER
WINTER GARDEN PLACE
GREENWICH PLACE
TWIN TOWER 1
TWIN TOWER 2
DEY STREET
CORTLANDT ST
CHURCH STREET
LIBERTY STREET

10 ↗

9-8 ↘

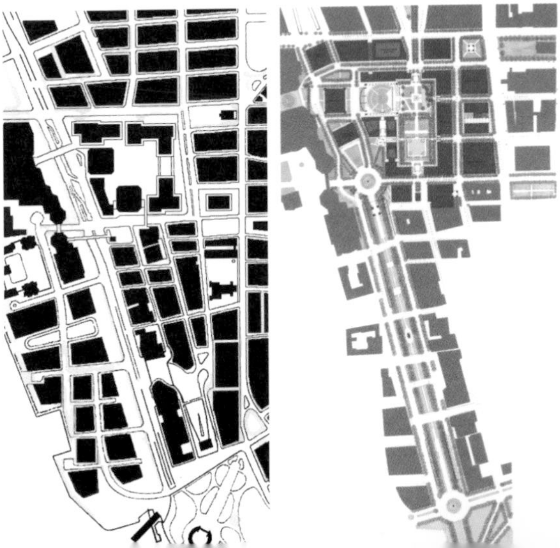

This is a photo of Grand Central Station and Park Avenue in an early phase of its development.[11] As the city expanded north, the grade-level rail tracks from the northern suburbs into the terminal were covered with a new, elevated avenue. The intersecting streets were connected east to west and a whole series of convenient, prestigious development parcels resulted. This precedent provided us with a goal to achieve the phasing and redevelopment of the site.

The model photo shows this idea quite literally applied to the site.[12] The garden as memorial can stand alone as an independently constructed element. It can have its own history, its own internal narrative and its own defining surfaces. Most importantly, it can precede the build-out of the commercial buildings which will depend on market demand.

The garden contains the World Trade Center plan inscribed in the earth. The south footprint is represented as a sunken pool of water. The sculpture of the world by Franz Koenig is returned to its original position at the cross axis of the two footprints recalling the towers formal relationship to each other. The placement of the memorial at the physical center of the site was critical to our scheme.

The north footprint is represented as an amphitheater to hold 2,800 people.[13] It is carved into the level of the garden and is enveloped in a semi-ruinous wall. A visitor could sit in the amphitheater and feel the expanse of the building that was once there with its uninterrupted acre floor plates. Individual seats would be dedicated to the individuals who perished in the attack, as they were to war dead in ancient times, again giving visual measure to the magnitude of lives lost. The memorial

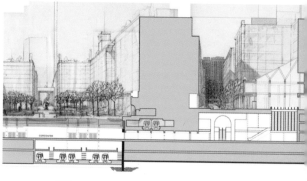

museum is located beneath the amphitheater and progresses down to bedrock.

The section is critical to establish the separate domains of memorial and city. We needed to create a sacred, protected, and meditative space in immediate juxtaposition with a vibrant renewed city.[14] New Yorkers longed for a return to the normality of daily life. The transition from city to memorial garden would be achieved via the wall of the garden itself and the layer of the buildings immediately around it. Lowering the garden from street level and locating portals on the extensions of existing streets would further reinforce the transition from one state of mind to another.

This is a model view looking down West Broadway terminating in the garden portal.[15] To the left is the parallel extension of Greenwich Street from the south, redirected on the dominant north-south grid. Named Greenwich Place, it is to be a new active shopping street leading to the underground PATH commuter station and terminating in a newly created Saint Paul's Square at Fulton Street.

This model shows a complete build-out of the site to its total ten million square foot capacity.[16] There are eighteen individual development parcels surrounding the garden, each of which can be a site for a unique piece of architecture. The parcels vary in size, some with small depth footprints for schools, housing and cultural institutions. Others are calibrated to receive standard market rate office buildings.

In this aerial rendering the new Greenwich Place and Saint Paul's Square are visible in the upper right.[17] The garden is surrounded by roof gardens serving the new office towers at the tenth floor sky lobby level. In the lower left

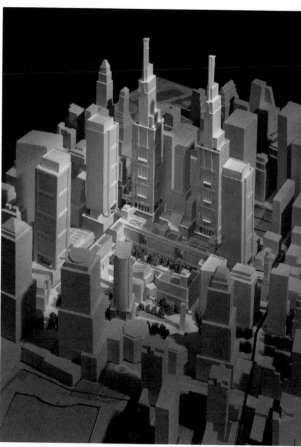

15 ↖

55

18 ↗

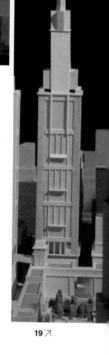

19 ↗

21 ↘

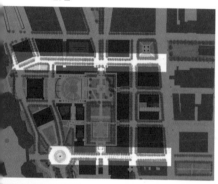

17C ↗

24 ↗

23 ↗

22 ↖

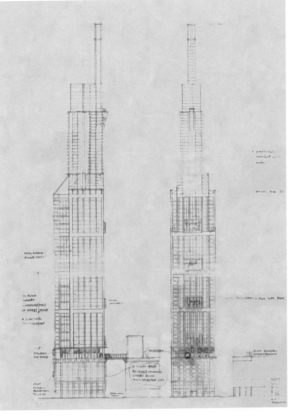

20 ↗

is Liberty Circle beginning the sequence down Memorial Boulevard, and marking the entry to Battery Park City.

A skyline view of the main two towers from the Hudson River.[18] They are positioned within the plan in a "checkerboard" with surrounding tall buildings to maximize open space and views at the upper levels.

The buildings themselves demonstrate the principals of the New York skyscraper, that is, they are layered vertically to respond to conditions both at the street wall and in the sky as independent towers.[19,20] Sky lobbies are located at upper level gardens overlooking the memorial. They establish a new ground plane, and help define the 110-foot street wall. Greenhouse structures are introduced in the towers above for positive environmental conditions. We hoped that housing or hotel could occupy the upper floors, resulting in a true mixed-use building.

The two critical east-west streets are highlighted, Fulton to the north and Liberty to the south.[21] They are re-established through the site as normative, two-sided retail streets, promoting connectivity across the island. Fulton Street connects the Winter Garden to South Street Seaport. Liberty Street is the primary entry to Battery Park City South and leads to the center of the financial district to the east.

An eye-level view down a rebuilt Liberty Street shows the obelisk marker at Liberty Circle.[22] It stretches active urban life to the door of Battery Park City.[23] The portal into the memorial garden is shown mid-block.[24] It punctures the street wall and serves as a transition to the incredible, quiet, garden place protected from the city within the block.

St. Paul's Square is proposed as a civic

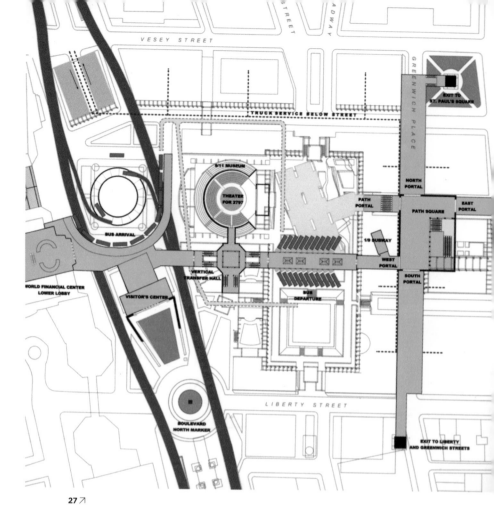

VESEY STREET

57

TRUCK SERVICE BELOW STREET

EXIT TO
ST. PAUL'S SQUARE

9/11 MUSEUM

THEATER
FOR 2797

NORTH
PORTAL

PATH
PORTAL

PATH SQUARE

EAST
PORTAL

BUS ARRIVAL

1/9 SUBWAY

WEST
PORTAL

WORLD FINANCIAL CENTER
LOWER LOBBY

VERTICAL
TRANSFER HALL

SOUTH
PORTAL

VISITOR'S CENTER

BUS
DEPARTURE

LIBERTY STREET

BOULEVARD
NORTH MARKER

EXIT TO LIBERTY
AND GREENWICH STREETS

GREENWICH PLACE

27 ↗

28 ↘

26 ↗

25 ↗

space that terminates the new Greenwich Place at Fulton Street. It marks the northeast corner of the World Trade Center redevelopment site.[25]

An aerial view of Liberty Circle at the southwest corner of the redevelopment site, which connects to the West Street promenade and is the main arrival point for memorial visitors.[26]

An underground plan shows the covered north-south bypass of West Street and the lower level east-west concourse, located midway between Fulton and Liberty Streets.[27] The bypass allows for bus drop-off, an area for service vehicle screening and entry to parking and the visitor's center. The concourse connects to the World Financial Center to the west and an underground shopping arcade to the east from the underground transit systems beneath the memorial garden.

Memorial Boulevard moves south along West Street.[28] We likened Memorial Boulevard to the Champs Elysée in Paris, which, not coincidentally, means Elysian Fields, an idyllic vision of the afterlife. It is part of a mile long sequence of public spaces stretching from City Hall Park, through the Memorial Garden, south to Battery Park and the landmarks in New York Harbor. This is intended as an innovative urban ensemble of true civic quality on a grand scale worthy of Manhattan as a world city.

It is interesting to compare this all with Daniel Libeskind's plan simply to illustrate how fundamentally different the two approaches are in regard to the idea of city.[29,30] His buildings come to the ground as literal architectural footprints. They don't conform to or construct urban blocks. There are no streets with two sides formed as urban spaces. There are paved paths that pass through plazas. On the other hand, upon close examination of all the other projects,

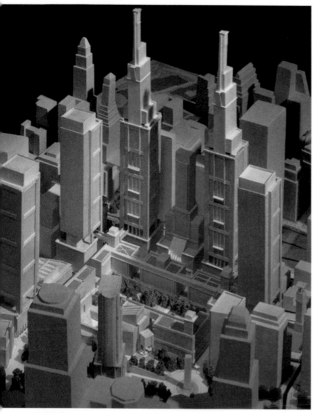

31-32 →

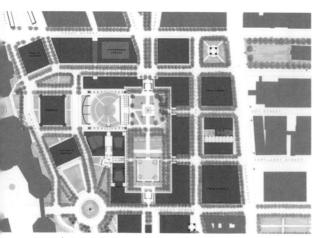

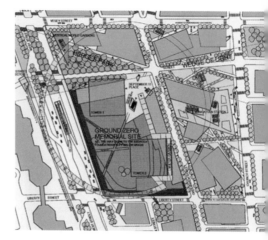

29-30 → Images 30 & 32 courtesy Studio Daniel Libeskind.

it becomes clear that his plan is actually one of the most urban.

Here is another comparison, the two models of the schemes in 3D.[31,32] Organizationally, they are radically different in plan and massing. One is a diagonal arrangement and the other orthogonal in plan. But, the towers and their positions are also based on a very different viewpoint. One emphasizes a single symbolic tower out on West Street, a freestanding, classically modern object. The other emerges out of and is integrated with the city grid. The towers form the coordinates of the perimeter of a space, while also reprising the symbolic idea of twin towers.

The final view looks down Memorial Boulevard, with the Statue of Liberty and Ellis Island seen in the distance from one of the new towers.[33]

Cities are able to contain different styles of buildings, which are part of the physical record of life, present and past. We believed, that only a complete urban fabric based on New York's traditional grid could heal this wound in all its complexity. The details are crucial. Vibrant city streets are not country roads. They need street walls to form them. Buildings with activities on both sides are necessary to generate vitality and energy. City blocks cannot be eroded by arbitrary setbacks and random empty plazas. There is a precision and rigor required to maintain city form and establish a permanence to the public realm.

33 ↘

Discussion

Peter Eisenman:
You make beautiful plans. They are better
plans than any New Urbanist. Your plan for
the World Trade Center was clearly the best in
terms of a good plan. The question is, is there
any validity today in the notion of a good plan?
People in their malls, in their cars, has their life
anything to do with a good plan?

The concept of a good plan is no longer
alive. It was in the plans of the nineteenth
century. But I do not think beautiful plans are
what cities are about today.

Barbara Littenberg:
I think you've aestheticized the idea of plan.
Granted, there are good plans and there are
bad plans. But a plan is simply a way of map-
ping and organizing space. I believe plans are
fundamental to suburbs and shopping malls,
as well as cities. Plans are necessary to organize
our physical environment – a good plan helps
people in malls find their cars. At its best a
good plan becomes beautiful and it takes on
the positive characteristics of form. Images
alone cannot adequately describe architecture
and the world we inhabit.

Steven Peterson:
The whole point of our project – let's call it
a "project" – was to put together an urban
structure at the ground level that contained a
major public space, not just a normative grid,
like the New Urbanists making new towns.
We re-wove the city together, healed it on the
ground, made a major public space, and then
on top of that put high-rise buildings, any kind
of towers you want. I could do one, anyone
could do one. It wouldn't make any difference.
It wasn't constructed in any historical sense as

being limited. All you had to do is put one of those six towers up to start. There are even two twin towers, like Norman Foster. Any architect could have done one of those little things on top of our urban plan.

Eisenman:

One could say that explanation sounds like Libeskind, who said anybody can do the towers. Norman Foster could do one, and you could do one. The operative word that you said is "heal the city." That means that you know what it takes to heal the city. You have within your wisdom and the work that you do – to heal the city. I do not know if I believe that. Who would not want to heal something. However, sometimes it is better to make wounds and let wounds stay. When I was in Berlin I felt that we should leave the wound of the wall as an artifact of the history of Berlin. Berlin wanted to cover it over.

Littenberg:

Libeskind essentially won on that premise, on leaving the Trade Center foundation wall exposed as a "wound." He agrees with what you said. Of course, despite all the drama of that idea it was the first thing to be eliminated by his client – it's no longer there, except as a minor incident.

Eisenman:

What I would question is whether you are correct that what you would do is healing, and that healing is necessarily a good thing.

Peterson:

Obviously, we thought it was a good idea because it was part of the plan.

Eisenman:

Recently I went out to Tulsa. I saw a grid that
looked like a bombed-out city. I said it was a
city of churches and parking lots, the buckle on
the Bible Belt. I said this city cannot continue
to grow. It has to contract, to make a fabric of
downtown. It needs a new kind of thinking
about urbanism, not going back to the way
Tulsa was in the twenties and thirties.

Today, one has to rethink Tulsa, rethink
Kansas City. One has to rethink many mid-size
towns that expanded after the War, when
everybody fled these towns to the 'burbs. When
Bill Gates says the shopping mall is a dead
issue, that means something has changed in
the pattern of growth. The interesting problem
for this country is not what do you do with the
New Yorks, Chicagos, etc., but what do you do
with the Tulsas, the Kansas Citys, the Detroits,
the St. Louis's where postwar growth has not
been sustained and the cities have emptied out.
Flint, Michigan, which used to be 300,000
people, is down to 180,000. What do you do
with the grid that sustained those places? That
is an interesting problem. How would one
restore something that is already in place that
is empty? How do you restore that emptiness?

Littenberg:

Maybe in those examples the emptiness can't
and won't be restored. Viable American cities
like Chicago and New York have been filling
up their emptiness through natural market development. I believe cities are very delicate ecological entities – each city has its own unique
problems and opportunities. Lower Manhattan
was particularly fragile and one had to handle
it with kid gloves. It is not Tulsa. It's not Flint.

I would argue for diversity of approach based on specific places and situations.

The world – despite what everybody's been saying in schools for the last twenty years, that cities are dead – is getting more and more urbanized. Cities will be built and they will take on new forms – no doubt about it. But I do not believe in rejecting the best aspects of city-making simply because it was done before. You speak of Piranesi and Nolli. I have those two maps on my wall, too. They are complex and intense and remain a constant source of ideas and inspiration for contemporary work.

Urban design, as a technique, must get involved with local physical conditions, history, and community, to achieve its goals. Some kinds of architecture seem to become global commodities. Work by Frank Gehry, Peter Eisenman – they are signature pieces that are autonomous and seem to adjust secondarily to their contexts. The creation of a true public realm which promotes an urban public life, urbanity itself, remains a valuable, desired thing in our cities and does not preclude the incorporation of unique architecture.

Eisenman:

I want to add one point. I do not agree with Steven's notion that architecture and urbanism are different. I would go back to Alberti's view that the city is a large house, and a house is a small city.

I do not believe that I am either an architect or an urbanist. We are all architects who deal with the problem of urbanism in the city.

I think you can make the distinction because, in my sense, the space between buildings is architecture, and how one deals with that space between buildings is an architectural problem. So I go on record as saying I don't accept that architecture and urbanism are separate.

Peterson:

If you do a building, which is architecture, you have to decide what it is. You get into these arguments about whether it is postmodern, avant-garde, Neoconservative; you get into the argument and you have to make a choice. It's a thing you're making. The thing about the city is that it contains all those things perfectly well without argument or pain. The city is a bigger form. On one side of one block you can have a modern building by Lescaze and on the other side have a neoclassical building by Charles Platt, and a stupid, ugly white brick building down at the end, and the continuity of the city works and the city contains them all – but only if you have a city.

If the city structure, the city fabric, goes away then you see each one of those things and they start fighting with each other. There is a subtle aspect to the reality of solid blocks made of multiple buildings. This is not theory. It's just what you experience. I'm not disagreeing with you that the street isn't also an architectural issue. However, the city is a different kind of form. It's made up of many architectures. In this sense, urban design is different from architecture.

Roy Strickland, moderator: Are there questions from the audience?

Questioner 1: For Barbara: You talked about the city having an identity. But it seems like the city, Lower Manhattan, was much more of a small, tight urban fit pre-9/11, and then you imposed a post-9/11 grid that was more Parisian. How do you make that kind of transfer to the identity of New York?

Littenberg:

Memorial Boulevard emerged directly from our 1994 plan. West Street was built to the specifications of an interstate highway for a misguided project planned in the seventies that has been abandoned because of community opposition. It exists now as a remnant, an oversized, uncrossable, spatial gap between Battery Park City and Lower Manhattan.

The Champs Elysée was an urban model that we drew upon – that is, a discreet piece of street with clearly marked beginning and end that was dedicated to war victims. The name is simply shorthand – in fact, it is more like Commonwealth Avenue in Boston, which has the pedestrian walkway down the center, de-emphasizing the building edges to either side. These are both useful precedents that also allow ordinary people to understand what you are talking about. To transform a highway wasteland into a unique street connecting the site of the tragedy to the monuments of New York harbor helped form a larger historical narrative for the expected masses of visitors to the 9/11 Memorial by enlarging the experience of the immediate site.

The formality of the garden derived from the geometry of the original towers, whose plans were in fact set at 90 degrees to each other, and followed the diagonal of the original shoreline. You can find the towers in the space as a kind of archaeology that also literally reveals the 18th-century shoreline in the northeast corner.

That is the design part of urban design, and I reject the notion that if you make a grid you're a New Urbanist. There is an art and technique to making these things meaningful and there are choices to be made and inventions to be discovered, which often breaks sets of rules. It becomes a living analytic and design process.

Peterson:
If you look carefully at the central memorial
garden in our project, there is no other public
space in the world made in this way. It's actually a huge rear yard for public use with a series
of buildings backing up to it. It is a unique
invention in a funny way, because it looks like
another normal public park in the renderings.
But it's actually a sort of hidden thing, which
one would not see overtly from the surrounding
streets. You can only get into it in three places.

We tried to produce a wide variety of
different places to memorialize 9/11 within
this new part of the city. Our idea about the
"boulevard" for instance was not that it was a
Parisian road but more like Commonwealth
Avenue, a linear park, centered on grass. Our
original idea was that this would actually
be the primary memorial, a space leading
from the World Trade Center site out to the
water and the ocean. It didn't fly because of
the families' and the public's fixation on the
former tower footprints. Political concern for
interpreting the family's collective thoughts
had an enormous impact on the whole process
of the World Trade Center design. This political caution is one reason it became a whole
mishigas. We don't have to bring this up, but
we all would probably agree.

The question becomes: Is it politically
possible to design or build any large-scale,
urban, public projects with real quality? It is a
quagmire of battles between public and private
interests, as well as the multiplicity of city,
state and federal agencies. You have to ask why
seven designs had to be made for this site.

Strickland: Another one or two questions from students?

Questioner 2: How important is public participation in the urban design process?

Peterson:

I think it's how the public participates. It's essential that the public not be thrown out of the process or to say that social and economic forces have no input. There is no reason not to involve the public in some way. However, the public in this case was snookered by the process, as were the architects, because they were led to believe they had something to say about it. They voted and went on line and did all this nonsense. Nobody paid any attention. They never even added up the votes. I know from inside who got the higher marks. They never announced it. They didn't pay attention to the public at all.

Eisenman:

I am suspect of public process. If we are doing a building at the University of Michigan. I would not want the students to vote. I do not think anything of value in architecture came about by people voting. I would not ever want some middle management bureaucrat running it either. I would probably go to the president where the buck stops and say, "Hey, we're going to do this together or not."

I have always believed that leaders are the people who lead, and architects should work for leaders and not listen to votes. I don't think Borromini ever listened to the people who went to church there.

Strickland: So, Barbara, no public voting on urban design projects?

Littenberg:

"Voting" on urban projects, as in any political process, must be based on real information and thorough understanding of the issues involved. As soon as a project affects a large public constituency or is larger than a single private building, you absolutely have to disclose to the public what's being proposed. That is one of the reasons I maintain that urban design must be local – sometimes the community has a real insight into the problem.

But you have to be on top of that process. We found when working with communities it's essential to understand the range of physical solutions first in order to share the thought process and show a range of ideas in diagrammatic and preliminary ways. Feedback can be incorporated into the design because it remains open ended, a work in progress. The architect is the only one who can put fragmentary components – formal, economic, programmatic, social – together into a coherent vision. It then becomes possible for people to coalesce behind a single solution.

When it works, when you bring different kinds of people with different interests together behind a plan, and they say they're all for it, it's wonderful.

Strickland: We've just had a question about the influences of technology and communication on urban design, do you have a comment?

Littenberg:

The implication of the question is that architecture and urban design have to reinvent themselves to accommodate new technologies. Perhaps all that is required is adjustment – electric light and telephones are earlier versions of technology and communication advances that totally transformed society. No one suggested then that you have to abandon all known forms of city design and building technique because of these.

I don't think we have to sit in agony boxes when we are at our computers, I would rather sit in a beautiful room. The relation of this activity to physical space is completely independent. Architecture is always looking for something external to its own discipline to find the next great inspiration and its reason for being. I don't buy into that.

Douglas Kelbaugh: I see a lot more complementarities and yin/yang between these two presentations tonight than might otherwise be evident.

Steve and Barbara, you talk about urbanism as something that simply exists, that's there, that is, like the weather. It's a container, it's a backdrop, it's a fabric, in which, and on which, architects do their thing — including Peter.

Peter seems to be talking about the foreground moves, the important, monumental buildings, which I would argue need a normative urban structure. You two need each other to be successful.

I have a question for both of you. Peter, the second project you shared, the West Side Yards, as well as your World Trade Center project, needed the normative, familiar fabric of New York to work. My question is how do we make and promote the new norms, the new standards for the city?

Peterson:

Well, just to come back to the World Trade Center site plan we did. There are ten or twelve blocks laid out on the site. The plan puts down the structure of blocks and streets; this street connects to that street. It's a grid integrated into the surrounding city. In a sense, there are no buildings yet, but there are building lots that are plenty big enough for anything you want. So you can have Rem Koolhaas build on one block, you can get Peter to build on another, and maybe out on the edge you can ask if Frank Gehry would build something. I don't want any of you doing the city plan. But it seems to me that this urban plan does not inhibit any of you. It is not ultimately a limitation on your "project."

This is what Herbert Muschamp misunderstands. He thought that if there were an urban design plan, everything would be automatically "nostalgic" with old-fashioned architecture. Unfortunately, maybe the renderings of our project buildings should have been done by some other architects. We didn't think of it in time.

Our idea was that the volumetric structure that we put down in space, in that place, was something rich and complex enough for anybody to work in. Muschamp gets it wrong, because he doesn't know what a city is. He thinks it's made up of ten or twelve contemporary architects whom he likes. It's unfortunate because it's a level of criticism and misunderstanding about our civilization and our culture and our urban condition that is limiting.

Eisenman:

There are two churches at the Piazza del Popolo, one on the left and one on the right. Both were worked on by Cario Rainaldi, but

the one on the left was corrected by Bernini to appear to be symmetrical in space when in fact it is not.

There is the contradiction between Bernini's idea of the relationship of architecture to space to the human viewer. The actual facts are corrected to give the viewer a sense of order and symmetry. So the facts are corrected. The Rainaldi church on the right is not corrected. There is a lesson for architecture and the relationship of architecture to urban space in the Piazza del Popolo.

One is not right or wrong. If you follow the Bernini line of discourse you are going to get to something more or less like the Peterson/Littenberg World Trade Center project. If you follow the Rainaldi line, which is an amalgamation of Palladio and Borromini, it is neither better nor worse. It is simply two opposing views. Wittkower summarized that in his article in 1935 on the difference between objective and subjective space. These two churches and the trident of streets have more to do with the relationship of building to urban fabric. The buildings are not just incidental in the Piazza del Popolo.

Peterson:

This is a very unique relationship of building to urban fabric, because these churches are meant to be an illusion, to appear to be objects. It's the conversion of the whole Roman urban texture down onto these points.

I prefer the Piazza Navona, where you also get a Borromini church, San Agnesse. However, this is perhaps more complex, because the church is imbedded into the long wall of the piazza. It is part of the space. The building is both an object of interest and a supporting constituent of the urban fabric.

Questioner 3: On your stance on urban design are you saying that your architecture has evolved over time, or that it does not change?

Littenberg:

My architecture, if anything, has become more respectful of place, be it the natural environment or the city. Architectural "evolution" itself is surely not limited by an urban plan, as evidenced by many older cities. But there are basic principals, or rules of behavior, which intimately connect city and building form independent of their style. Cities derive much of their character, their texture, from the underlying assumptions about the scale of the building produced, from an economic standpoint. For example, the Trade Center site, which was this huge thing assembled by eminent domain, was completely different in scale from the surrounding context. This resulted in an urban disconnect that did serious damage to the neighboring fabric.

Sites have become larger and larger because they are cheaper to develop. New York has been transformed from a predominantly town house city to one of a much coarser scale where small sites are combined to produce bigger and bigger buildings. We deliberately made smaller sites at the World Trade Center to question this trend toward gigantism.

When you are dealing with new towns in places like Asia, the urban plan depends on the nature of an assumed architectural result. If there is no civic structure or history that's guiding these kinds of developments, anything goes (for better or worse).

Peterson:

Let me say, I think there is a limit to how far you can modify the essential urban elements. City form, once you take certain things away, will fall apart. You don't have city form any more. If Le Corbusier's Towers in the Park are inserted as a substitute for the fabric of Paris, you don't have urbanism. It's gone. You have buildings standing around with no way to get to them except across a vast open space or through a park. You don't have streets, "the horrible streets," he called them. If you take away certain constituent elements of city fabric or city form, you don't have "city."

Cities do evolve and develop in various ways, just like there are lots of different kinds of cheese. The differences in character between Paris, Rome, London, Florence, and New York are distinct, but in an essential way they remain the same. They all have streets, and various kinds and shape of blocks. They all have a mystery to them. They all have an extended fabric, which is somewhat independent of the architecture, which occupies it. It's hard to describe, but I think there is a separate temporal continuity to urbanism from its buildings.

Look at Lower Manhattan. What was it? It was a 400-year evolution, with recent additions, and replacements.

There are also places like downtown Detroit, which have had so many buildings taken away that it doesn't seem to exist as a city anymore. Yet, strangely, the streets are all still there. Downtown Detroit still has a fragmentary, palpable memory of its past inscribed on the ground.

Questioner 4: When you design projects, how do you rationalize keeping the wounds instead of healing the city? Is urban design necessary? Do we need to be engineering such large projects?

Peterson:

I don't know. We can't help but keep trying. We will always have visions of sugarplums in our heads. When there is a piece of a city in transition or a problem in the city, we can't help ourselves. It's probably like Peter reacting to a new theory, we have go in there to try to figure it out or devise a neat way to improve it.

Littenberg:

I'll be a utopian as a conclusion. Look at Central Park. Any time a city can get it together to achieve a great civic intervention like that, it is truly an extraordinary occurrence. Yes, cities will build themselves. They will probably do it in the most aggressive and base way economically. That's where the issues of community and public good come up, and they are very important issues to make urban life bearable.

I must say working to improve areas in the public, common domain – the streets, parks, squares, etc. – is to achieve something that sometimes we take so much for granted. Making a park in a city – for hundreds of years it changes people's lives. It has value far beyond the life of an individual work of architecture. I think that's where innovative design comes in. It has to do with intentionality, from a public point of view, and I think that is what's missing in the current architectural discourse.

Questioner 5: As for the Rem Koolhaases of the world, there is a sense of the architect as hero, which seems to me very real to students. Going to places like Asia and Africa where others have not gone also makes him accessible to students. I'd be curious to hear from you folks about diversity.

Eisenman:

I believe that Koolhaas' books on the Pearl River Delta and Lagos trivialize the problem of diversity. They turn a serious problem into a comic book format – easy, light reading – and not much real analysis. In a debate, Cornell West charged Koolhaas with trivializing the problem of ethnicity by the kind of research that he was doing; it is both not serious and cynical.

For students, those Taschen books look great and they are easy to walk around with, and you do not have to work too hard to get the message. The problem of diversity cannot be trivialized in a Taschen book.

Peterson:

Maybe I have too much faith in the city as a condenser, but it seems to me that you need to provide a complex set of spaces in which diversity will occur. The juxtaposition of groups, functions, and activities needs to take place spatially, in close proximity. The people that do various things bump into each other. Out on the highway strip, in the malls, you have to get in the car and go from one place to another. You can avoid one another. In the city, multiple levels of economics, race, culture and functions can happen within the same block structure. It is arranged in such a way that it can all be there together, without having to offend the other. Because you are ever-present to each other, it builds up this acquaintance.

In our two blocks on Lexington Avenue there is a Russian deli, a grocery run by a couple who are Iranian and Russian, a police station, a fire station, a church, a synagogue...

You need "city." New York was planned. It didn't just happen by the grace of God.

Strickland: We just had an interesting question. Can you plan that diversity?

Peterson:

It happens. You can make the space to allow it to happen. You're not going to get it unless you have density and congestion.

Eisenman:

Planned spaces don't make those things happen. The street makes it happen. New York was planned when someone laid out a grid in the nineteenth century. That was planning.

Roy Strickland, Director of the Master of Urban Design Program at Taubman College, formerly directed the Urban Design Program at Columbia University and chaired the S.M.Arch.S. Committee at MIT. His authored works include *Between Party Walls: Nineteenth-Century New York Residential Architecture and Urbanism* in *Rethinking the 19th Century City,* and *Designing a City of Learning,* recipient of the 2002 EDRA/Places Award.

Urban Design and War Without End

To help set the context for this book – and the practice of American urban design – we must contemplate a state of affairs that was incomprehensible only four years ago: perpetual war. Because Al Qaeda's demands on the United States appear non-negotiable – among them, abandoning Israel, withdrawing troops from the Middle East, and paying more for the region's oil (Anonymous, xviii) – the nation's cities, centers of economy and culture, are targets for attack for the foreseeable future.

In response, security agencies and consultants are reconfiguring the American city to both subtle and profound effect. In Chicago, granite bollards clog Miesian free space. In Washington, jersey barriers make L'Enfant's radials an obstacle course. In New York, concrete flower planters obscure Park Avenue's Modernist transparencies. Around major targets everywhere, sand-filled dump trucks are the new urban gateway. The results can be shattering (Washington's Mayor Williams asking how his city can conduct business and survive) or sublime (the temporary closing of streets approaching the United Nations revealing the Corbusian cityscape's full power for the first time).

In order for urban designers to assert themselves into this post-9/11 landscape, they will have to address the realities of American urban life that is less stable, convenient, and free than in the recent past. They will have to subdue fear by providing urban pleasures in target-rich environments (such as walking through a traffic-free United Nations). And they will have to suggest processes that will generate new symbols of community that will deepen people's commitment to their cities in the face of catastrophic danger.

More than fifty years ago, Hugh Ferris, the great mid-twentieth century architectural delineator, portrayed apocalypse in Piranesi-like drawings of underground shelters vast enough for mass transportation, housing, and airports. These were the architectural equivalents of post-World War II film noir, perennially dark and shadowy, ominous in their suggestion of life post-nuclear holocaust. He asked, "Can the blueprints be drawn, and is the money forthcoming? Will real estate interests allow the razing of wide swaths of valuable property for any purpose whatever? Will the populations of large cities join in an orderly, gradual exodus to scattered communities, or will they take a chance on a last-minute final route? Will people live underground?" (Ferris, 49)

The blueprints were drawn and the money was forthcoming, if not for Ferris' underground bunkers then for the other half of his vision: a suburban boom that was part civil defense strategy as public and private interests sponsored highways and low-cost mortgages to move populations from central cities. (Plunz, 277) What settlement patterns will emerge from the current crisis? The answer will determine whether the elegant projects presented in this book influence the future of urban design or recede as artifacts of the past.

References

Anonymous. *American Hubris: Why the West is Losing the War on Terror.* Washington: Brassy's, 2004
Hugh Ferris. *Power in Buildings.* New York: Columbia University Press, 1953
Richard Plunz. *A History of Housing in New York City.* New York: Columbia Univesity Press, 1990

Contributors

George Baird is Dean of the University of Toronto's School of Architecture, Landscape and Design and a partner in Baird Sampson Neuert Architects in Toronto. He is the co-editor (with Charles Jencks) of *Meaning in Architecture,* the author of a book on Alvar Aalto, of *The Space of Appearance,* and the forthcoming *A New Theory of Public Space.*

Peter Eisenman, principal in Eisenman Architects, has won numerous design awards and taught at Princeton, Harvard, Yale, Cambridge, and Ohio State as well as founding the Institute for Architecture and Urban Studies in New York. He is author of several books, including *House X, Fin diOu T Hous, Moving Arrows, Eros and Other Errors,* and *House of Cards.*

Douglas Kelbaugh, Dean of Taubman College of Architecture and Urban Planning at the University of Michigan, has won a score of design awards and competitions, organized and participated in thirty design charrettes, and taught at eight architecture schools in the US and abroad. In addition to writing dozens of articles, he has edited and authored several books, most recently *Repairing the American Metropolis: Common Place Revisited.*

Barbara Littenberg is a founding partner of Peterson/Littenberg Architecture & Urban Design and visiting professor at Yale School of Architecture. Since 1979, she has been responsible for the firm's award-winning design work ranging from private houses to urban design projects. The firm was an invited entrant into the international competition for the World Trade Center Site.

Steven Peterson, a founding partner of Peterson/Littenberg, has a forty-year involvement with urban design and city planning. He was Assistant Chief Deputy Architect for Milton Keynes New Town in England, executive director of the Institute for Architecture and Urban Studies in New York, and director of the Syracuse University Post-Professional Program in Architecture in Florence, Italy.

Roy Strickland, Director of the Master of Urban Design Program at Taubman College, formerly directed the Urban Design Program at Columbia University and chaired the S.M.Arch.S. Committee at MIT. His authored works include *Between Party Walls: Nineteenth-Century New York Residential Architecture and Urbanism* in *Rethinking the 19th Century City,* and *Designing a City of Learning,* recipient of the 2002 EDRA/Places Award.